The Library of Explorers and Exploration

LA SALLE

Claiming the Mississippi River for France

Simone Payment

the rosen publishing group's
rosen
central

Published in 2004 by The Rosen Publishing Group, Inc.
29 East 21st Street, New York, NY 10010

First Edition

Library of Congress Cataloging-in-Publication Data

Payment, Simone.
La Salle : claiming the Mississippi River for France / by Simone Payment.— 1st ed.
    p. cm. — (The library of explorers and exploration)
Summary: Profiles the explorer who, upon hearing rumors of the Mississippi River, determined first to find it, then to claim it for France and establish French settlements from Canada to the Gulf of Mexico.
Includes bibliographical references and index.
ISBN 0-8239-3628-7 (lib. bdg.)
1. La Salle, Robert Cavelier, sieur de, 1643–1687—Juvenile literature.
2. Explorers—Mississippi River Valley—Biography—Juvenile literature. 3. Explorers—France—Biography—Juvenile literature.
4. Mississippi River Valley—Discovery and exploration—French—Juvenile literature. 5. Mississippi River Valley—History—To 1803—Juvenile literature. 6. Canada—History—To 1763 (New France)—Juvenile literature. [1. La Salle, Robert Cavelier, sieur de, 1643–1687.
2. Explorers. 3. Mississippi River—Discovery and exploration.
4. America—Discovery and exploration—French.
5. Canada—Discovery and exploration—French.]
I. Title. II. Series.
F352 .P29 2002
977'.01'092—dc21

                                                    2002002037

Manufactured in the United States of America

CONTENTS

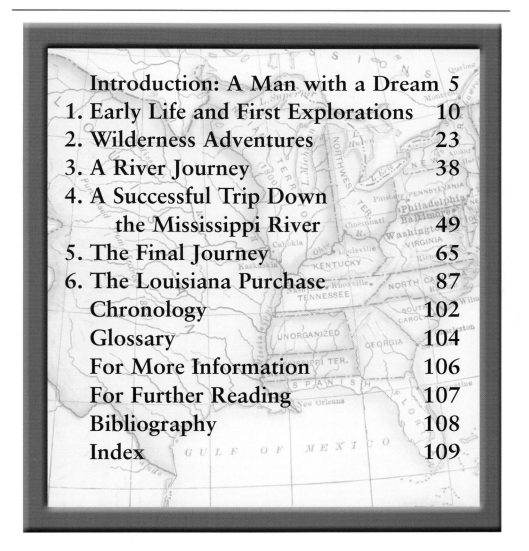

Sieur de La Salle immigrated to Canada in 1667. There, he became obsessed with discovering a legendary route to Asia through central North America. Over the years, some people saw him as a visionary, while others questioned his sanity because of his obsession with becoming a successful discoverer.

INTRODUCTION

A MAN WITH A DREAM

If you wanted to find the Mississippi River today, you could look at a map, check the Internet, or even use a global positioning system (GPS). Then you could get in a car, on a train, or on a plane and head for the river. But what if you lived in the 1600s and you weren't even sure the Mississippi River existed? There were no maps of the Mississippi back then. There were no computers or global positioning systems. There were no cars or trains or planes to get you there. You would have to use your own two feet or a canoe. If you were René-Robert Cavelier, Sieur de La Salle, you wouldn't let that stop you.

The French-born La Salle was about twenty-five years old when he first heard stories about a huge river that led to an ocean. Native Americans he met near his home in Canada told him about the river, but they couldn't tell him how to get there. La Salle wasn't sure how to find it, and he didn't even know for sure that it existed. That didn't matter to La Salle. For him, the river was a mystery, and finding it would be an adventure.

At first, La Salle believed that if he could find the Mississippi, it would lead him to the Pacific Ocean and China. Explorers had been trying to find an easier way to sail to China for more than a hundred years. In China, they could buy spices, silks, precious stones, and metals. At the time that La Salle was born, European ships sailing westward had to go around the southern tip of South America to reach China. It was a long and dangerous journey, and French sailors had to worry about being attacked by Spanish ships. The only other route to China was a difficult trek over mountains or around the tip of Africa and across the Indian Ocean, around India.

After a few years of exploration, La Salle learned from other explorers that the Mississippi River did not lead to the Pacific Ocean. Instead, he later discovered, the river led to the Gulf of Mexico. His new dream was to set up a French empire in North America that would stretch from Canada to the Gulf of Mexico. He wanted to claim control of the Mississippi for France and establish French settlements along the river. Then they could begin trading and send goods back to France. La Salle planned to bring explorers and mapmakers to the area first, then soldiers and traders, and finally people to set

This French map of the Mississippi River from 1766 details some of the tributaries that feed into the Red River. Until the mid-twentieth century, the Red River flowed into the Mississippi. With the construction of a flood-control system, however, the Red River ceased to supply water to the Mississippi.

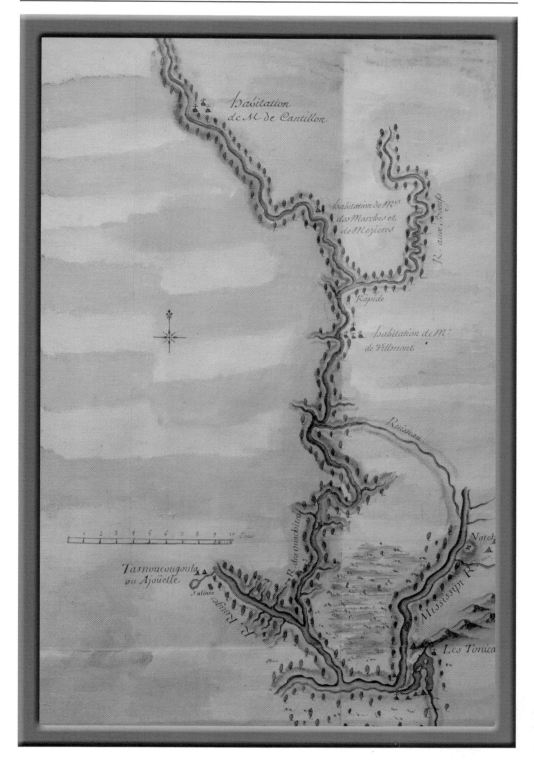

up villages and farms and stores. La Salle's plan was a good one, but he didn't have the money and supplies to carry it out. He didn't have support from other people in Canada. His neighbors in Montreal just wanted to stay where they were, trade with local Native Americans, make money, and maybe go back to France one day. But La Salle worked hard all his life to make his dream come true.

Most explorers wanted to find gold and treasure or bring glory to themselves or their countries. While La Salle was interested in those things, he chose to be an explorer because he enjoyed pushing himself to the limit. Throughout his life, many people thought La Salle was crazy. They could not understand his dreams and plans. They could not figure out why he would want to travel in the wilderness for years at a time. But what other people thought was not important to La Salle. He did not have many friends. He was shy and very serious and had a hard time getting to know other people.

Some of these characteristics made him a successful explorer. They also caused him a lot of trouble. He was not always a good leader. He upset people with his unwillingness to take advice or suggestions. People sometimes thought he was rude, and many people didn't like him. People who did like and understand him were very loyal to him. Henri de Tonti was one such man. He called La Salle "one of the greatest men of this age, a man of admirable spirit."

8

La Salle did not have an easy life. He spent years alone in the wilderness pursuing his dream. Along the way, he suffered many setbacks. He lost his land, his money, his ships, and, in the end, his life. But La Salle did fulfill part of his dream. He sailed the length of the Mississippi, proving that it reached the Gulf of Mexico. In 1682, he claimed the Mississippi and all the land surrounding it for France.

Although La Salle's discoveries were misunderstood at the time, they have become very important to the United States. The Mississippi River is one of the most important waterways in the world. The land La Salle claimed (later called the Louisiana Territory) would eventually become about one-third of the United States. It stretched from Canada in the north to the Gulf of Mexico in the south and from the Mississippi in the east to the Rocky Mountains in the west. The purchase of the Louisiana Territory from France in 1803 helped to turn the young United States into a great power respected throughout the world.

1
EARLY LIFE AND FIRST EXPLORATIONS

The life I am leading has no other attraction for me than that of honor; and the more danger and difficulty there is in undertakings of this sort, the more worthy of honor I think they are.

—La Salle

René-Robert Cavelier, Sieur de La Salle, developed a taste for adventure early in his life. As a young boy, he would go to a bridge near his house and watch boats heading out to sea. He dreamed of sailing on one of the boats, maybe on a whaler or fishing boat. As he grew older, he began to dream of finding a shorter sea route to China.

La Salle was born in Rouen, a town near Paris, France, on November 21, 1643. He was the second son of Jean Cavelier and Catherine Geest. His father was a wealthy businessman. He owned a large estate named La Salle. This is why King Louis XIV later gave Robert the title "Sieur de La Salle." It means "gentleman from La Salle."

La Salle's birthplace, Rouen, is a port city eighty-four miles northwest of Paris on the Seine River. Although it sits seventy-five miles inland, Rouen was an outport (a seaward terminal for deep-draft vessels) of Paris before World War II. Industries have now replaced the ports at Rouen and include chemical works and plants that make mechanical equipment, cars, and aircraft parts.

Studying with the Jesuits

La Salle went to a very good school where he was taught by Jesuits. The Jesuits are an order of Catholic priests. They are very religious and are excellent teachers. La Salle was a good student and did especially well in math. He learned about English, French, and Italian explorers who had "discovered" new lands in what are now

The First Canadian Settlers

The first settlers from France had gone to live in Canada more than a hundred years before La Salle arrived. Most had gone there to trade beaver, deer, fox, and rabbit furs with the Native Americans. The furs were sent back to France, where they were made into hats and other warm clothing.

The fur trade was an easy way for the settlers to make money because fur was plentiful. Even so, not many people went to live in Canada. France was busy fighting a war in Europe and was not too interested in Canada. After the war was over, more people moved to Canada when France offered people free land there.

Canada and the East Coast of the United States. He studied hard and was preparing to be a priest just like his teachers. But even as a schoolboy, La Salle was restless. He thought more and more about exploring.

When he was seventeen, La Salle entered a Jesuit college where he learned about math, geography, astronomy, and navigation. After three years at college, he started teaching school. Soon he decided that he could not wait any longer to begin exploring. He wrote a letter to the Jesuit priests in March 1666 asking for permission to go to China. The priests refused, but La Salle was not yet ready to give up. He tried again in December, but the priests still would not allow him to go to China. He grew impatient, and a few months later, he decided to leave the Jesuits.

While La Salle was trying to leave the Jesuits, his father died. He left a large amount of money to La Salle and his other children. However, because of Jesuit rules, La Salle wasn't allowed to use any of the money he had inherited. His brothers and sisters agreed to give him a small allowance, but he would have to find a way to earn extra money. La Salle's older brother, Jean Cavelier, was a priest who had gone to Montreal, Canada. La Salle decided to follow him there and seek fortune and adventure in Canada.

Adventure in a New Land

La Salle sailed to Canada in 1667. He was twenty-three years old and eager to start a new life. He bought land on an island a few miles away from the rest of the settlers in Montreal. La Salle enjoyed being by himself and clearing his new land. He built houses and a fort for protection. To make money, he rented some of his land to new settlers. He also made money by trading furs.

As he settled into his new home near Montreal, La Salle began to explore the area. He met Native Americans who lived nearby and began learning their language and customs. La Salle learned a great deal from them about the land and the animals that lived in the area. He would later put this knowledge to good use.

Two years after he arrived in Montreal, some Seneca Indians came to visit him. They stayed with him for the whole winter and told him stories about the Ohio River. In their language, "Ohio" meant "beautiful." They told him that this huge, beautiful river led to the sea. This excited La Salle. Could this be the river he had dreamed of finding that might lead to China? Historians are not sure if the river the Senecas told him about was the river we call the Ohio River today, or if it was the Mississippi River. As La Salle would later find out, neither river would lead him to China.

14

The demand from Europeans for fur from the New World exploded in the 1600s. European animals were dying out because of overhunting, and popular new fashions, such as hats, used great quantities of felt and fur. The fur trade led to the establishment of many settlements in Canada.

La Salle Prepares for His First Expedition

After La Salle's visit from the Seneca Indians, he began to plan a trip to search for the river they had told him about. He was eager to begin an adventure. In 1669, he went to Quebec, a city near Montreal, to discuss his plan with the governor. He needed permission to look for the river, and he hoped to get money to help him on his mission. The governor was interested in the plan. He knew some missionaries who

15

were also looking for a river that would lead to China. The governor decided that La Salle should work with the Jesuits to find the river. However, the governor decided that La Salle would have to pay for the trip himself.

In order to buy the canoes and supplies they would need, La Salle had to sell his land to other settlers in Montreal. With the money, he bought four birch bark canoes and supplies. He found fourteen men to go along. La Salle also found some Seneca

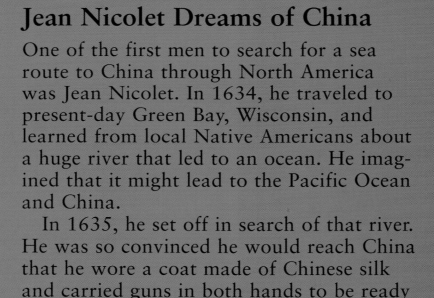

Jean Nicolet Dreams of China

One of the first men to search for a sea route to China through North America was Jean Nicolet. In 1634, he traveled to present-day Green Bay, Wisconsin, and learned from local Native Americans about a huge river that led to an ocean. He imagined that it might lead to the Pacific Ocean and China.

In 1635, he set off in search of that river. He was so convinced he would reach China that he wore a coat made of Chinese silk and carried guns in both hands to be ready to meet Chinese royalty. Instead, he found the Winnebago Indians. They threw a party for him and served 120 roasted beavers.

This painting depicts the landing of Jean Nicolet (1598–1642) on the Wisconsin shore of Lake Michigan in 1634. Jean Nicolet was a French explorer who came to New France with Samuel de Champlain in 1618. In 1634, under the direction of Champlain, he took a voyage west in search of the Northwest Passage to China, exploring Lake Michigan, Green Bay, and the Fox River. He was drowned on a trip to Trois-Rivières in New France.

Indians who agreed to go along as guides. He bought corn, blankets, gunpowder, and other ammunition and loaded up the canoes.

The Adventure Begins

On July 6, 1669, La Salle set off on his first journey with the missionaries and their Seneca guides. The missionaries wanted to teach the Native Americans they met about their religion, which was Christianity. They hoped that the Native Americans would become Christians.

17

We know a lot about La Salle's first mission because one of the missionaries, Father Galinée, kept a diary recording their journey. He also made a map of their travels. His diary tells us how they traveled, where they slept, and what they ate. It was a difficult, tiring journey. They paddled the canoes down the Saint Lawrence River all day long. Sometimes they had to carry the canoes when the water in the river was too low or if there was something in their way. They slept on the ground around a fire. If it rained, they peeled bark from a tree and put it over a frame made of sticks. They ate crushed corn boiled with fish or meat. By the time they were just a few hundred miles from Montreal, all of the explorers were sick.

After two months on the Saint Lawrence River, La Salle and his group reached Lake Ontario. They followed the southern shore of the lake. After eight days, they met some Seneca Indians near what is now Rochester, New York. The Senecas invited them to visit their village. There were about 150 huts made of bark with a tall wooden fence surrounding the village. The Senecas treated them well at first, sharing many feasts of pumpkins, berries, and dog meat. La Salle and his men were given a large hut to stay in. But about a week after they arrived, the Senecas captured a Native American from an enemy tribe. La Salle watched in horror as the Senecas tortured, burned, and then ate the prisoner. It was time to leave the Seneca village!

La Salle and his men returned to Lake Ontario and continued their journey. Soon they reached Niagara Falls and had to take their canoes out of the river and walk. They arrived at an Iroquois Indian village. There they heard that there were many Native Americans in the area who were eager to be converted to Christianity. This was not true, but the missionaries believed it and they decided to stay in the area. La Salle did not want to stay. He wanted to continue his search. He lied and told the missionaries that he and his group would return to Montreal. As soon as the missionaries left, La Salle told his group that they were going to continue on. Joining them on their journey was Nika, a young Shawnee Indian from what is now Ohio. The Iroquois had been keeping him as a slave. La Salle bought Nika from the Iroquois, and he became a guide and faithful friend to La Salle.

The Lost Years

No one is sure what happened to La Salle and his men next. No records or diaries survive to tell us exactly what they did or where they went for the next two years. Many historians believe that during the first winter, the rest of La Salle's men left him and stole his supplies. La Salle decided to continue anyway. He enjoyed working on his own and was happy to get rid of the missionaries and the rest of his men.

Quebec is seen across the Saint Lawrence River in this image. In 1608, French explorer Samuel de Champlain founded a settlement and trading post along the Saint Lawrence River that eventually became the city of Quebec. It was the first permanent European settlement in Canada. Although New France began with the founding of three cities—Quebec City in 1608, Trois-Rivières in 1616, and Montreal in 1642—it eventually included territories that extended west in what is now the United States to the Ohio and Mississippi Rivers.

La Salle, alone except for Nika, probably traveled the rivers and lakes in the area and stayed with Native Americans along the way. Some historians believe La Salle actually discovered the Ohio River during this time. Maps made a few years later show the Ohio River and describe it as "the river discovered by the Sieur de La Salle."

No one from Montreal went looking for La Salle during the two years he was gone. Even his brother thought La Salle was a little crazy. But this is when La Salle got his real education. He learned how to rely on himself and how to survive in the woods. Native Americans he met taught him how to hunt and fish. He learned more Native American languages and customs. The time La Salle spent with them also reinforced his love for exploration.

2
WILDERNESS ADVENTURES

We must suffer all the time from hunger; sleep on the open ground, and often without food; watch by night and march by day, loaded with baggage . . . sometimes wading whole days through marshes where the water was waist deep or even more, at a season when the snow was not entirely melted.
—La Salle, describing the trip to Fort Frontenac

In 1671, after two years in the wilderness, La Salle returned to Montreal. His neighbors thought it was strange that he had been trying to find China. They nicknamed the land that he used to own "La Chine" (which means China in French). La Salle did not let this bother him. He was already busy planning his next trip. He was eager to explore again and claim land for France.

In the summer of 1672, La Salle went to speak to the new governor of Canada. The governor's name was Louis de Buade, Count of Frontenac, and he was very interested in what La Salle had to say. La Salle told the governor he had some new information from Native Americans, and he now believed the Mississippi would lead to the Gulf of Mexico. He planned to

Frontenac

claim the land around the river for France. He wanted to build forts along the Mississippi where the French could trade furs with the Native Americans. He also planned to build a large fort at the end of the river. There they could attack the enemy Spanish settlers in the Gulf of Mexico.

Count Frontenac was very excited about this plan and wanted to help La Salle. First, however, he needed some help from him. The Iroquois Indians were beginning to cause trouble for the French settlers. Frontenac knew that La Salle had become friendly with many Native Americans during his travels. He sent La Salle to meet with the Iroquois to try to get them to discuss their problems with Frontenac. La Salle was successful, and Iroquois leaders met with La Salle and Frontenac on June 3, 1673. The Iroquois signed a treaty with Frontenac that allowed the French to build a fort on Lake Ontario. La Salle was in charge of constructing this fort. He named it Fort Frontenac in honor of the governor. When it was completed, La Salle began trading furs with the Native Americans and making money for himself and Frontenac.

Louis de Buade, Count of Frontenac, was born on May 12, 1620, at Saint-Germain-en-Laye, France. He served as governor general and representative of Louis XIV in New France from 1672 to 1682 and from 1689 to 1698. He died in Quebec City on November 28, 1698. In Canada, Frontenac is considered the architect of French expansion into North America and the defender of New France against attacks from the Iroquois and the British colonies.

Now that La Salle had helped Frontenac, they were ready to put their plan into action. La Salle was eager to begin because news of Louis Jolliet and Father Jacques Marquette's journey on the Mississippi had reached him. Because of their expedition, it was now known for certain that the Mississippi led to the Gulf of Mexico. Frontenac decided to send La Salle to France to talk to King Louis XIV. La Salle would try to get permission for the first steps of their plan.

La Salle began the long boat trip across the Atlantic Ocean to France in 1674. He carried with him a letter from Frontenac telling the king that La Salle was "a man of intelligence and ability" and one

Jolliet and Marquette Discover the Mississippi

Two other French explorers made it to the Mississippi before La Salle. Louis Jolliet and a Jesuit missionary named Jacques Marquette were chosen by the French government to find the Mississippi in 1673. They reached the river on June 15 and traveled about 1,100 miles of the Mississippi. They went as far as the Arkansas River. Convinced that the Mississippi flowed into the Gulf of Mexico, they returned to Montreal to report their discovery.

Louis XIV was only four years old when he became king of France upon the death of his father, Louis XIII. Though power was initially seized by his minister, Cardinal Mazarin, Louis regained control in 1661. Louis reorganized the administration and finances of the kingdom, and he developed trade and manufacturing. Louis also reformed the army and racked up military victories, and he encouraged an extraordinary blossoming of culture, including theater, music, architecture, painting, sculpture, and all the sciences. Louis XIV is sometimes called the Sun King because he chose the sun as his emblem.

of the most competent men he knew. When he arrived, La Salle headed straight for Louis XIV's palace. He stayed at the palace that winter talking with the king. Finally, the king agreed to the first step of La Salle's plan. On May 13, 1675, he made La Salle governor of Fort Frontenac. La Salle was given all the land surrounding the fort, as well as the official title "Sieur." In return, La Salle would have to pay France back for what it cost to build the fort.

Success at Fort Frontenac

A few weeks later, La Salle returned to Montreal. He told Governor Frontenac what King Louis XIV had decided. Then he quickly left for Fort Frontenac. By September, he had taken control of the fort. He built housing for soldiers, a bakery, a mill, and large boats to carry supplies on Lake Ontario. He cleared land for farming and began trading with the Native Americans. Fort Frontenac was very successful and became a center of the fur trade.

La Salle's success at Fort Frontenac made people in Montreal jealous. To make things more difficult for La Salle, they started holding supplies that were supposed to go to him. They told the Iroquois that La Salle was planning to attack them. They wrote to France to complain about him and told the king he was crazy. One man even poisoned La Salle; he was sick for a month but recovered. He didn't let any of this stop him. He still dreamed of reaching the Mississippi.

Another Trip to France

Now that Fort Frontenac was successful, the governor decided to send La Salle back to France. Once again, he began the long ocean journey. He left September 7, 1677, and by May 1678, La Salle had permission from King Louis XIV to begin searching for the Mississippi. He was allowed to set up forts along the river. The forts would belong to La Salle. There were a few conditions, however. La Salle had to complete his mission in five years. He had to pay for all his explorations by himself. Also, he was not allowed to trade with any Native Americans who would normally trade in Montreal.

La Salle was very excited. He was finally going to put his plan into action. First he had to raise money for the trip. He began asking friends and family members to help him. He promised to pay all of the money back, with interest.

While he was in France, La Salle met a man who would become very important to him. The man's name was Henri de Tonti. He wanted to go with La Salle on his search for the Mississippi. At first, La Salle was not sure if that was a good idea. Tonti had lost one of his hands when a grenade exploded near him. In place of his hand, he wore an iron claw covered with a glove. But Tonti quickly showed La Salle that he was very skilled and made up for his physical disability with bravery and intelligence.

29

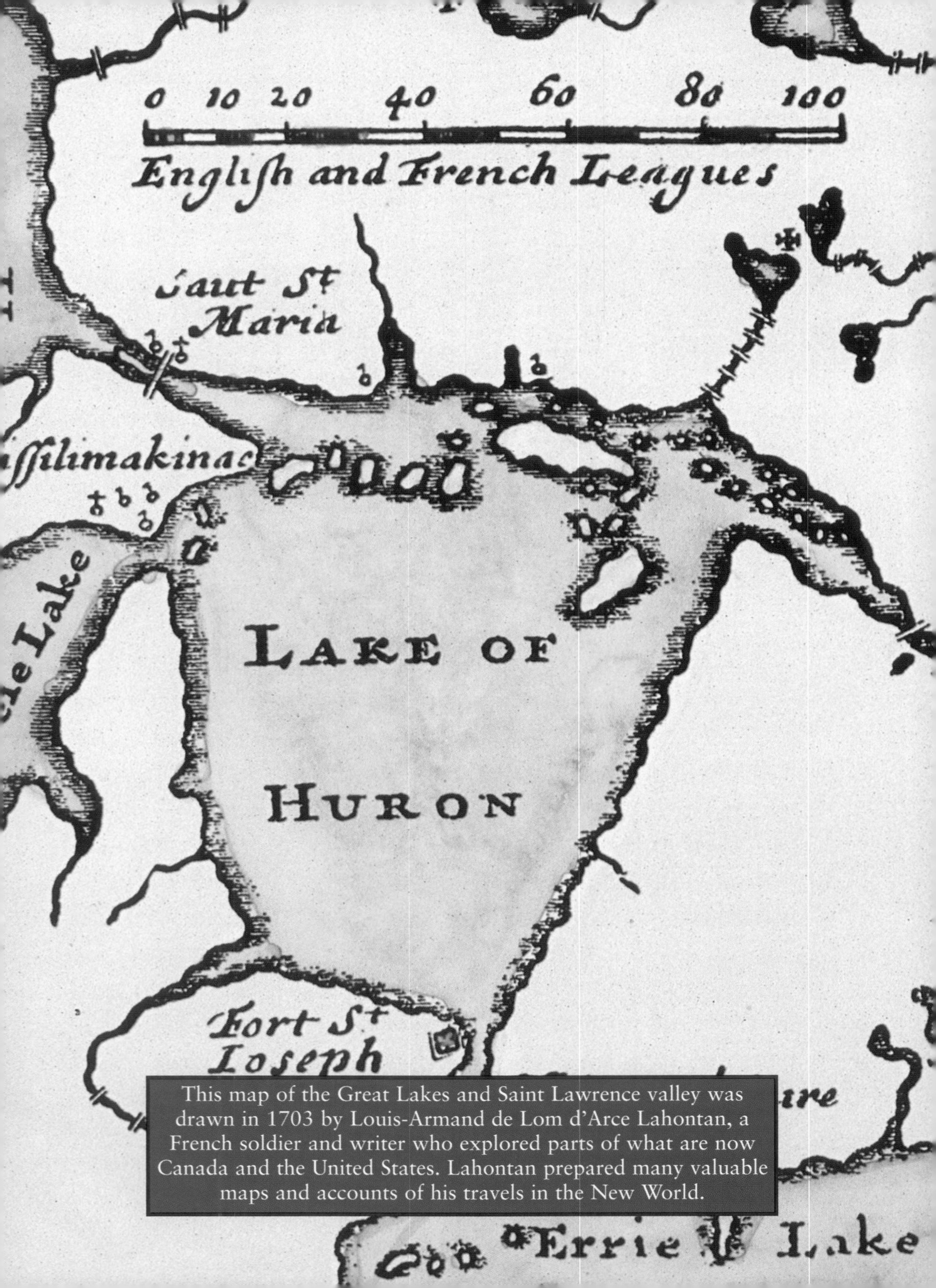

0 10 20 40 60 80 100

English and French Leagues

Saut St
Maria

ssilimakinac

e Lake

LAKE OF

HURON

Fort St
Ioseph

This map of the Great Lakes and Saint Lawrence valley was
drawn in 1703 by Louis-Armand de Lom d'Arce Lahontan, a
French soldier and writer who explored parts of what are now
Canada and the United States. Lahontan prepared many valuable
maps and accounts of his travels in the New World.

Errie Lake

The *Griffon*: First Step of the Plan

With Tonti, thirty men, and supplies, La Salle headed back to Montreal on July 14, 1678. He had decided that the first step would be to build a huge ship to sail the lakes and rivers he planned to travel. He brought supplies such as anchors, sails, ropes, and other materials that were hard to find in Canada. He also took carpenters, ironworkers, and pilots to help build and sail the ship.

As soon as the men and supplies reached Montreal, La Salle sent them to the Niagara River on the other side of Niagara Falls to begin building the ship. La Salle stayed in Montreal to raise money to buy more supplies. In the early fall of 1678, La Salle and Tonti went to join the shipbuilders on the Niagara River. They soon received bad news. A boat that had been bringing supplies they would need to build the huge ship had sunk in the Niagara River. Only some anchors and ropes were saved. Father Louis Hennepin, a missionary who was part of La Salle's group, later wrote that the loss of the supply ship "would have made any one but [La Salle] abandon the undertaking."

That was not the end of bad news. In the fall, La Salle heard that people back in Montreal wanted to be paid back the money they had lent him. They did not believe his mission would succeed. La Salle knew he would need to take care of this situation. He needed to convince them they would get their money back. So he set

Louis Hennepin was a Franciscan missionary who wrote the first published description of New France (Canada). Hennepin joined La Salle in Canada in 1675 and became his chaplain in 1678. They reached the site of Peoria, Illinois, in January 1680, where they established Fort Crèvecoeur. La Salle returned to Fort Frontenac for supplies while Hennepin and the rest of the party explored the upper Mississippi River. In April, they were captured by Sioux Indians and traveled with them to what is now the site of Minneapolis, Minnesota. Hennepin was rescued by another French voyager in July 1680. Hennepin returned to France in 1682 and wrote an account of his exploits.

off for Fort Frontenac in February 1679. He went on foot, taking two men and a sled. The three men walked 250 miles over frozen ground, pushing themselves through the snowbanks. They had only one bag of dried corn, and it ran out two days before they reached Fort Frontenac. When he reached Montreal, La Salle told the people who had lent him money that they would be repaid. He got more supplies and turned around to make the trip back to the Niagara River.

La Salle and his men sailed the Great Lakes in search of the Mississippi River, encountering dangerous weather along the way.

While La Salle was away, the men had been working on the ship. They cut huge trees near the river and used the tools and supplies they had brought with them. Because there was one in his family's coat of arms, La Salle named the ship the *Griffon*. A griffon is a mythical beast with the body of a lion and the head and wings of an eagle. The *Griffon* was soon finished and set sail on Lake Erie on August 7, 1679. La Salle, Tonti, Father Hennepin, and thirty other men celebrated the launch of the ship with the Native Americans who lived nearby. The Native Americans were impressed with the *Griffon*. They had never seen a ship that large and were amazed by how quickly it had been built.

The *Griffon* sailed across Lake Erie in just a few days. Then it sailed across Lake Huron. The *Griffon* almost sank in a storm while crossing the lake but reached a small fur trading settlement safely. The settlement was called Michilimackinac. La Salle had sent some of his men ahead to make friends with the Native Americans who lived there. He had given the men gifts for the Native Americans. Instead, the men had traded the gifts for furs and brandy. They had kept the furs and brandy for themselves and disappeared.

La Salle decided to leave Tonti at Michilimackinac to look for the men. La Salle and the others continued their

Michilimackinac was established by the French in 1673 as a trading post, becoming Fort Michilimackinac in 1715. In 1760, during the French and Indian War, the fort was taken over by the British. In 1763, a band of Chippewa-Sauk Indians destroyed the fort and massacred its inhabitants. In 1780, the British moved the fort across the straits to Mackinac Island. The village of Michilimackinac was laid out in 1857 and its name was shortened to Mackinaw in 1894.

journey on the *Griffon*. They crossed Lake Michigan and found some other men who had been sent ahead. The men had already obtained a large amount of furs. La Salle decided to send the furs back to Fort Frontenac on the *Griffon*. The furs would be used to pay his debts to the people who had loaned him money. Meanwhile, La Salle's journey in search of the Mississippi continued.

3

A RIVER JOURNEY

[La Salle was the] most tragic figure in the history of Mississippi exploration. Of all the Mississippi explorers he had the greatest vision, the most meteoric career, and the worst luck.
—Timothy Severin, from *Explorers of the Mississippi,* 1967

Determined to continue his mission at any cost, La Salle loaded canoes with men and supplies and set off in September 1679. The men faced many storms and they lost many of their supplies and guns. Many of the men nearly drowned. By November 1, 1679, they arrived at the Saint Joseph River, where they had planned to meet Tonti. But Tonti and the twenty men he was leading were a few weeks late. While they waited, La Salle and his men built a small fort called Fort Miami. Soon Tonti arrived with supplies and they were ready to continue.

Although most of La Salle's expeditions ended in failure, his explorations were landmarks. He was responsible for opening the Mississippi valley for development, and his entry into the Gulf of Mexico sparked a renewal of Spanish exploration in the entire gulf region. His attempts at setting up a colony there gave the French a claim to Texas and led to the Spanish occupation of eastern Texas and Pensacola Bay. Because of La Salle, the United States was able to register a claim to Texas as part of the Louisiana Purchase.

On December 3, 1679, the group started down the Saint Joseph River in eight canoes. They floated down the river through forests, marshes, and plains. There was not much food. The men were very hungry and were growing impatient with La Salle. One day they came upon a buffalo trapped in a swamp. They managed to get a rope around the buffalo. It took twelve of the men to drag it out of the swamp. The buffalo meat kept them from starving.

The men continued down the Saint Joseph in search of the Kankakee River. They believed the Kankakee would take them to the Mississippi. They thought they were close, but they could not find the river. Nika, La Salle's Shawnee Indian guide, knew how to find the river but he was away on a hunting trip. La Salle tried to find it on foot while the others stayed with the canoes, but he got lost in a snowstorm in the woods. He came across a small camp with a fire still burning. No one was around so La Salle decided to stay for the night. He wasn't sure if he would be safe, so he built a small fence of dried branches in a circle around him. If anyone came to attack, the sound of the dried branches would alert him. La Salle slept, and when he awoke the next day, he was glad that he had built the fence. A ring of footprints in the snow around the fence told him that someone had been near. He found his way back to Tonti and the others. Nika, who had returned from his hunting trip, led them all to the Kankakee River.

Once La Salle and his men found the Kankakee River, it was a short trip to the larger Illinois River. While they traveled down the Illinois River, they met many Native Americans. Some were unfriendly and tried to scare the men with lies about the Mississippi. They told the men that the Mississippi was full of giant lizards and snakes, evil spirits, and demons. La Salle didn't believe them, but some of his men did. Six of them chose to leave. Others tried to convince La Salle to turn back, but he refused. One man even poisoned La Salle's dinner, but La Salle took some medicine and recovered. Once again, people had tried to stop La Salle, but he was determined to continue.

Bad News

The winter weather was making travel difficult, so La Salle decided to stop and build another fort. He named this new fort Crèvecoeur, which means "heartbreak" in French. The men built the fort and then began building another ship like the *Griffon*. La Salle had received some bad news about the *Griffon*. The ship had never made it back to the Niagara River with its load of furs. No one had seen the ship.

While his men were busy building the fort and another ship, La Salle sent Father Hennepin down the Illinois River to

La Salle was the earliest European explorer to visit the Saint Joseph River, and he called it the Miami River for the Miami Indians he met living along its banks. The Potawatomi Indians who lived in the area called the river Sheggwe, which means "happened spontaneously." This name came from a legend of a man who would mysteriously materialize on Saint Joseph's banks.

begin exploring the Mississippi. Tonti and six-teen men would remain at Fort Crèvecoeur. La Salle, Nika, and four other men began a trip back to Fort Frontenac to look for the *Griffon* and get supplies for the new boat. They left Fort Crèvecoeur on March 1, 1680, and faced a terrible trip in the cold, damp weather. Even though La Salle knew the trip would be difficult, he decided to travel by foot to Fort Frontenac to find out what had happened to the *Griffon*.

After about eight days of walking, they arrived at Fort Miami on Lake Michigan. There the bad news about the *Griffon* was confirmed. The ship had never arrived. They were now sure it had sunk. All the valuable furs on board were lost as well.

After a few days of rest, they left Fort Miami. La Salle wrote: "The rain lasted all day and the woods were so [full of] thorns and brambles that in two days and a half our clothes were all torn and our faces so covered that we hardly knew each other." The rest of the journey was just as difficult. They met some unfriendly Native Americans along the way, but each time La Salle was able to make friends with them.

It took La Salle and his men sixty-five days to travel the 1,000 miles back to Fort Frontenac. They finally arrived on May 6 and left soon after for Montreal. People in Montreal were surprised to see them. They had not expected La Salle to return and had been selling off his property to pay his debts. La Salle paid off the rest of his debts, quickly gathered supplies, and began the trip back to Fort Frontenac and on to Fort Crèvecoeur.

More Bad News

When La Salle reached Fort Frontenac on July 22, 1680, a letter from Tonti was

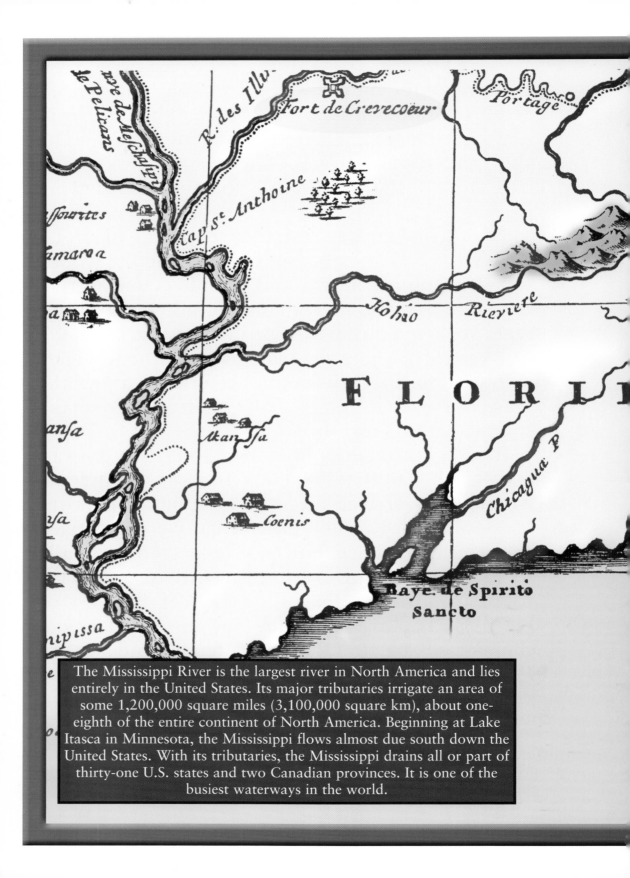

The Mississippi River is the largest river in North America and lies entirely in the United States. Its major tributaries irrigate an area of some 1,200,000 square miles (3,100,000 square km), about one-eighth of the entire continent of North America. Beginning at Lake Itasca in Minnesota, the Mississippi flows almost due south down the United States. With its tributaries, the Mississippi drains all or part of thirty-one U.S. states and two Canadian provinces. It is one of the busiest waterways in the world.

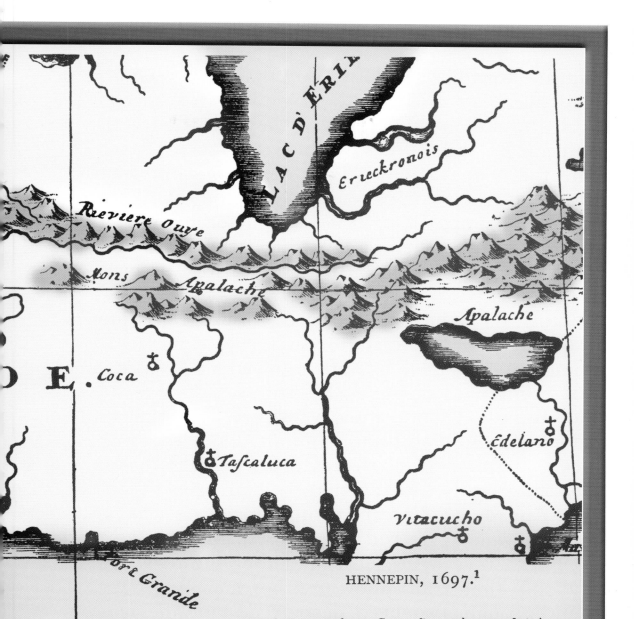

HENNEPIN, 1697.[1]

[1] Extract from *Carte d'un très grand pais nou-vellement découvert dans l'Amérique septentrionale, entre le Nouveau Mexique et la Mer glaciale, avec le Cours du Grand Fleuve Meschasipi . . . à Utreght.* The same plate was used for the editions, *à Leiden,* 1704, etc. The plate was re-engraved with English names for the English editions.

waiting for him. The letter said that the men who had been left at Crèvecoeur had destroyed the fort and stolen the supplies. They had done the same at La Salle's forts on the Saint Joseph River and the Niagara River. They had stolen the furs stored at Michilimackinac and were on their way to Fort Frontenac to kill La Salle. Luckily, La Salle and nine men from Fort Frontenac captured the approaching men on Lake Ontario. The men were quickly arrested.

Now La Salle was worried about Tonti. He hurried back to the Illinois River to find out if Tonti was all right. La Salle and twenty-five men left Frontenac on August 10, 1680. They reached the Illinois River in early winter. They were shocked to find an Illinois Indian village that had been completely destroyed by Iroquois Indians. All the Illinois Indian villagers had been killed. Their heads were on the ground or up on stakes. La Salle was upset and worried. He continued on to Fort Crèvecoeur. He found that the fort and the ship that Tonti and the other men had been building had also been destroyed. La Salle was happy to find that Tonti did not seem to be among the dead. They decided to look for Tonti along the Illinois River.

La Salle discovers that Fort Crèvecoeur had been destroyed and his men had been killed.

La Salle's troubles were piling up. He had lost the *Griffon* and had almost been killed by his own men several times. He had lost his land back in Montreal. He and his men were facing another difficult winter in the wilderness. Tonti, his loyal friend and assistant, was lost or perhaps dead. La Salle felt alone, but he was not ready to give up.

The cold winter trip along the Illinois River took a toll on La Salle. By the time they reached Fort Miami, La Salle was very sick. He and his men had to spend six months at Fort Miami while La Salle recovered. While they were there, La Salle began planning his next attempt to sail down the Mississippi. He also got to know many of the Native Americans who lived in the area. La Salle realized that it would be important to bring Native Americans with him on his next journey.

The Native Americans also had some good news for La Salle: Tonti was still alive! He was living with Potawatomie Indians near Lake Michigan. As soon as La Salle was well enough, he took his canoe up Lake Michigan to find Tonti. After they were reunited, La Salle and Tonti left for Montreal. They were on their way to tell Governor Frontenac about the plan for their next attempt to find the Mississippi.

4

A SUCCESSFUL TRIP DOWN THE MISSISSIPPI RIVER

I take possession of this country of Louisiana, the seas, har-
bors, ports . . . all the nations, peoples, provinces, cities, towns,
villages, mines, minerals, fisheries, streams, and rivers.
—La Salle's speech at the mouth of the Mississippi River

La Salle and Tonti reached Montreal in the fall of 1681. La Salle spent a few months discussing his new plan with Governor Frontenac. La Salle had decided that his next journey would focus on exploring the Mississippi. He would worry about building forts later. He prepared his supplies and found French settlers and Native Americans to make the trip with him.

Finally all was ready, and in December 1681, La Salle, Tonti, a missionary named Father Membré, twenty-three Frenchmen, and twenty-five Native Americans began their journey. The rivers they had planned to travel were frozen, so they had to journey by foot. They piled their canoes, tents, pots, blankets, tobacco,

guns, and axes onto sleds. The group followed the frozen Illinois River, walking about 120 miles over the snowy ground. When they reached the Mississippi in early February, they found that it was still frozen. They waited a few days near the river until one morning the ice began to crack. Soon the ice melted, and they lowered their canoes into the fast-moving river.

Finally, the Mississippi River

At long last La Salle was on the Mississippi. The journey began February 13, 1682. Compared to La Salle's previous journeys, this one was easy. He and his men were able to find plenty of food, and the French and Native Americans worked well together. They hunted for buffalo and cooked the meat by digging a hole in the ground and filling it with layers of hot stones, leaves, vegetables, and meat.

By March 12, La Salle had reached the Arkansas River. This is where Father Jacques Marquette and Louis Jolliet had turned around eight years earlier.

Soon after they passed the Arkansas River, fog crept in. La Salle and his men were unable to see the shore of the river. The sounds of drumbeats

La Salle and his companions explore the Mississippi River in canoes.

and a Native American war cry came from one bank of the river. They quickly headed for the other bank of the river and began to build a fort for protection. When the fog disappeared, they saw Native Americans on the other shore. The Native Americans were just as surprised to see La Salle's group. La Salle rowed out into the river and met the Native Americans with a peace pipe in his hand. La Salle's years of living with and learning from Native Americans paid off. The Native Americans recognized the peace pipe as a sign of friendship. These Native Americans were called Quapaws, and the tribe welcomed La Salle and his group. They helped them make huts, shared their food, and celebrated.

During the visit with the Quapaws, La Salle placed a cross on their land. He held a ceremony to claim the land for King Louis XIV of France. As La Salle set up the cross, he and his men shouted, "Vive le roi!" which means "long live the king." Father Membré preached to the Quapaws, and all the men fired their guns in celebration. It is likely that the Quapaws did not understand what La Salle meant, but they enjoyed the ceremony anyway. They were curious about the white men and their weapons. They probably did not understand that La Salle was claiming land they lived on for a king who was thousands of miles away.

La Salle and his men most certainly trapped beavers, as seen above. European explorers used many different kinds of traps, including snares, which would trap the animal in a wire noose, and baited traps, which would attract the animal with food. Native Americans commonly used the deadfall trap, which dropped a heavy weight onto the beaver to kill it. Traps had to be checked often to ensure that other animals would not eat the captured prey.

Their peaceful meetings with Native American tribes continued as they made their way down the river. In each village, La Salle performed a ceremony claiming the land for France. The Native Americans welcomed them and shared their food. Along the way, La Salle's group had killed bear, buffalo, deer, turkeys, swans, and geese for food. As they made their way south, food was harder to find. They began to kill and eat alligators. Soon, even the alligators were growing scarce. One day as they floated down the Mississippi, they saw three Native Americans in a canoe. As they came closer, the Native Americans got scared and left their canoe. When La Salle and his men looked inside the canoe, they saw bones. The explorers were hungry, so they devoured the meat. Immediately, they knew they were eating human flesh.

Who Saw the Mississippi River Before La Salle?

By the time people from Europe arrived in North America in the late 1400s, Native Americans had already been living near the river for thousands of years. In 1541, the Spanish explorer Hernando de Soto may have been the first European to discover the southern part of the Mississippi. He was looking for gold and pearls and was also looking for a water route from the Gulf of Mexico to the Pacific Ocean. De Soto and other Spanish explorers did not find treasure or a water route, so they lost interest in the river. No European explorer saw the Mississippi again for about 130 years.

A few days later, they reached a place where the river split into three branches. La Salle decided that he and some of his men would take the west branch. He sent Tonti down the middle branch, and another assistant took the east branch. Each group soon reached the Gulf of Mexico. At that moment, La Salle became the first man from Europe to travel most of the length of the Mississippi River. La Salle was almost forty years old, and he had been waiting nearly fifteen years for this day.

La Salle Claims the Mississippi

After a few days of exploring the end of the river and the Gulf of Mexico, La Salle and his men went back upriver to find a high spot on which to set up a cross. On April 9, 1682, they found the perfect place and cleared the land by cutting down all the trees. They made a cross and put it in the ground with a sign that read: "Took possession of this land in the name of Louis XIV, king of France." La Salle put on his finest clothes. He wore a red coat decorated with gold lace, silk stockings, and shoes with gold buckles. La Salle had brought the clothes all the way down the Mississippi in a trunk so that he would be ready for this special day.

La Salle claims the Mississippi River for Louis XIV, king of France. The discovery of the mouth of the river gave France the right to claim both the river and the land drained by its tributaries. La Salle and Governor Frontenac hoped for a French occupation of the entire Mississippi valley by building military posts. The French would then be able to control the communication and sway the policy of the Indian tribes, as well as present an impassable barrier to the English colonies. The plan eventually worked out, although not in La Salle's lifetime.

La Salle made a speech claiming the Mississippi and all of the land around it for France. He named the land Louisiana in honor of King Louis XIV. La Salle did not know how large this area was, but it turned out to be three times larger than the whole country of France. It was made up of all the land that today is divided into the states of Arkansas, Colorado, Iowa, Kansas, Louisiana, Minnesota, Missouri, Montana, Nebraska, North Dakota, Oklahoma, South Dakota, and Wyoming, as well as all of the land east of the river up to the Appalachian mountains.

Finally, La Salle had proven what he had believed for years: The Mississippi River flowed all the way to the Gulf of Mexico. The river could connect older cities like Montreal to the newer forts that the French hoped to set up along the Mississippi. This was important because the river and the forts would keep the English settlers living along the east coast from expanding their settlements farther west. The new French settlers would be able to use the land for farming. They also hoped that they could mine silver and gold.

La Salle understood the strategic significance of the Mississippi River's huge drainage system when he claimed the entire Mississippi basin for France. Within a generation, the Mississippi River became a vital link between France's settlements in the Gulf of Mexico and Canada, and La Salle's claim was designated as "Louisiana." La Salle's companion, Franciscan missionary Louis Hennepin, drew this map of the Mississippi River valley.

The Return Trip

Once La Salle had finished his ceremony claiming the land, there was nothing left to do but turn around and head back to Montreal. La Salle's group began to run into trouble, however. Because they had to row against the current of the river, it was a slow trip. Also, they had little food. They had been living on potatoes and alligator meat, but as they went farther north, they could not find many alligators. They thought they had had a little luck when they met the Quinipissas Indians near the Red River. The Quinipissas gave them 200 pounds of corn in exchange for knives, tobacco, and axes. That night, however, the Quinipissas Indians attacked the explorers. La Salle and his group were able to hold them off with guns and escaped the next morning.

As they continued their trip back to Montreal, La Salle became very sick. He was near death for forty days. The expedition had to stop at a small fort they had built on the way south so he could recover. They spent months there while La Salle regained his strength.

Father Membré stayed with La Salle at the fort. Tonti and some others left to get the news of their discovery to the governor. By September 1682, La Salle had recovered enough to continue the trip. He joined Tonti at Michilimackinac, but Tonti

French trading posts like Fort Saint Louis, seen above, did an impressive fur-trading business and forged strong relations with the native peoples of the area.

had some bad news for him. While La Salle had been sailing on the Mississippi, his friend Governor Frontenac had been forced to leave Canada. There was a new governor, and he did not like La Salle. The governor was planning to take all of La Salle's forts away from him.

Tonti had more bad news. The Iroquois Indians were getting ready to attack the Illinois Indians and La Salle's forts. They were angry that they were being cut out of the fur trade. La Salle decided he would have to go back down the Illinois River to the place where a fort called Starved Rock had stood. He

61

La Salle built Fort Saint Louis at Starved Rock, a steep cliff some 125 feet above the Illinois River, just south of Lake Michigan. He quickly established a colony of a small core of French colonists and several thousand Indians from the region. La Salle sought assistance from Quebec to help sustain the new colony. Frontenac, however, was no longer in office and the new governor ordered the surrender of Fort Saint Louis. La Salle refused to do so and is seen here leaving Fort Saint Louis for France to appeal to Louis XIV. The king sided with La Salle and ordered the governor to return La Salle's property.

would rebuild the fort that had been destroyed a few years earlier. There the French and nearly 6,000 Illinois Indians could defend themselves.

The new fort was finished in the spring of 1683. La Salle renamed it Fort Saint Louis. It was built on a high rock near the Illinois River, near where Chicago is now located. La Salle and his men planted corn around the fort so they would have food to eat later in the year.

La Salle set up Fort Saint Louis as a fur-trading center so he could make money to get out of debt when he returned to Montreal. His five-year contract with the king was running out. La Salle wrote three letters to the new governor but received no response. Then he discovered that the furs he had been sending to Montreal had not been arriving. La Salle realized he had better hurry back to Montreal. He left Fort Saint Louis in August. Only thirty-five miles up the Illinois River, he was met by thirty canoes sent by the new governor. They were on their way to take over Fort Saint Louis. La Salle was ordered to return to Quebec immediately.

5

THE FINAL JOURNEY

We had imagined that the king would send us two or three ships. But after having waited for years, we did not know what to think. Sometimes . . . we imagined that the king . . . had forgotten all about us.
— Jean Cavelier, writing about being lost in Texas

La Salle's situation looked bad. He did not have much money. He no longer had the support of the governor. Most of his friends and neighbors in Montreal were against him. They did not understand the importance of what he was trying to do. But, as usual, La Salle had a new plan. He was not sure he would be able to put it into action. None of this worried La Salle. He knew what he had to do. Once again La Salle would have to make the long trip to France to talk directly to the king.

In November 1683, La Salle and Nika began their journey to France. They arrived late in December. They faced the difficult task of convincing the king of their new plan. King Louis XIV liked La Salle, but

La Salle's adventures in the wilderness of the New World were the talk of Paris, and he was received as a hero by the court of Louis XIV. La Salle's request for assistance had the benefit of perfect timing: King Louis XIV was fighting with Spain, and he lept at the chance to establish a base on the Gulf of Mexico to strike at his enemies. He ordered La Salle to return to the New World and set up a fort to secure the lower Mississippi River. He was to then prepare for an attack on Spanish colonies.

many people back in Canada had tried to turn him against the explorer. The king had begun to believe them. Also, he was not sure that the discovery of the Mississippi was important. He wrote, "I am convinced that the discovery of the Sieur de La Salle is very useless."

A New Plan

La Salle's new plan was to sail across the Atlantic Ocean and into the Gulf of Mexico. He would set up a fort near the southern end of the Mississippi River. France would then control the river, the land around it, and the Gulf of Mexico. This was important because it would prevent Spain from gaining control of the area. France was at war with Spain and wanted to have every advantage it could. La Salle told the king that the fort they set up could be a port for ships that could take riches from the new land back to France. The location of the new fort would also allow them to attack the Spanish silver mines in the area.

Finally, in March 1684, the king agreed to La Salle's plan. He gave control of the forts along the Mississippi back to La Salle. He also gave La Salle command of the troops that would accompany him. And the king gave him permission to set up a French colony at the southern end of the river.

To make the journey, La Salle needed money, supplies, men, and ships. La Salle got two ships from the king: the *Joly* and the *Belle*. He raised money to buy two more ships: the *Aimable* and the *Saint François*. Now he needed sailors to sail the four ships. People with skills such as carpentry were needed to help build the fort. Soldiers were needed to defend it against the Spanish. Once again La Salle ran into trouble. Since France was at war with Spain, there were few soldiers available to go with him. In addition, the men La Salle sent out to find skilled workers were not choosy enough. Once the laborers were put to work, it became clear that they had no skills at all.

The Ocean Journey

Finally, the four ships were ready. They were loaded with food, live animals, guns, ammunition, and building supplies. On board were La Salle, his brother Jean Cavelier, his nephew Moranget, Nika, 100 French soldiers, craftsmen, and a few women and children. The group set sail on July 24, 1684.

By 1684, La Salle had established an extensive colony on the Illinois River. He hoped to build a fur-trade empire there, but the colony disintegrated not long after his death.

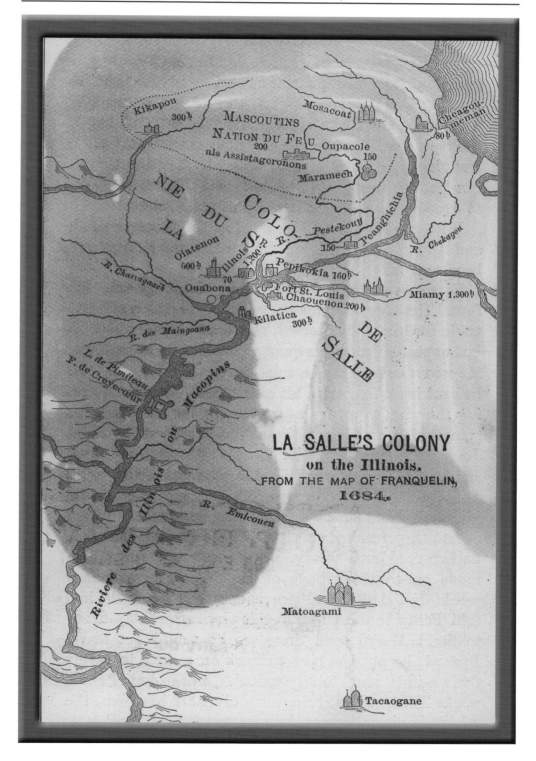

LA SALLE'S COLONY
on the Illinois.
FROM THE MAP OF FRANQUELIN,
1684.

Right from the start they ran into trouble. The largest ship, the *Joly*, had to return to France for repairs. All the other ships had to return, too. When they left France again, La Salle almost immediately began arguing with the captain of the *Joly*. Captain Sieur de Beaujeu had been placed in control of the voyage by the king. La Salle was not used to being a follower, and he was impatient with Beaujeu. La Salle thought he was better than Beaujeu. Also, he did not trust Beaujeu. Beaujeu thought La Salle was too secretive about their plans and didn't know much about sailing. The two men fought all during their journey south across the Atlantic.

By the time they reached the Caribbean island of Santo Domingo, there was even more trouble. Spanish pirates captured the *Saint François* and stole all of the supplies on the ship, including valuable tools. Additionally, La Salle became very sick with a serious fever. The group was forced to spend a few months on the island while he recovered. In November, they were ready to head for the Gulf of Mexico. By the end of December, they reached the Gulf and saw land. La Salle was sailing on the *Aimable*, which got separated from the *Joly*. When the two ships finally met up again in early January, they were already 400 miles past the Mississippi.

Lost in the Gulf of Mexico

No one is sure why La Salle missed the Mississippi. Maybe it was a simple mistake. Without accurate maps, La Salle was relying on the measurements he had made when he had sailed down the Mississippi two years earlier. The measurements could have been wrong. Also, the Mississippi is very difficult to see from the Gulf. There are three main mouths and many smaller ones. There are no good landmarks such as trees or hills to point it out from the sea. Another possibility is that he passed the Mississippi on purpose so that he could get closer to the Spanish silver mines in Mexico. Whatever the reason, La Salle and his group were now lost.

In addition to being lost, many of the people on board the three ships were sick and hungry. They had few supplies left, so La Salle decided to go ashore and try to find out where they were. We know now that La Salle's three ships were in Matagorda Bay, about eighty miles from present-day Galveston, Texas. But La Salle had no idea where he was.

According to journals kept by Minet, an engineer on one of the ships, on January 20, 1685, La Salle rowed ashore in a small boat but returned later that night "very tired, having found only lakes and marshes." The people on board the

ships were worried and hungry, and some begged La Salle to turn around and try to find the Mississippi by sea. But La Salle was stubborn and told them that he knew what he was doing and that they could go home if they wanted. Minet wrote to La Salle and begged him to turn the ships around. La Salle refused.

Setting Up a Fort

By the end of February, La Salle had decided that he and his men should go ashore. He believed that the *Aimable* should enter the bay to get closer to land. But, adding to their troubles, the *Aimable* got stuck on a sandbar and began to sink. The men unloaded flour, corn, meat, brandy, and wine into smaller boats, but a storm prevented them from saving most of their supplies. They lost many tools and weapons and a lot of food and medicine.

The situation did not improve on land. Captain Beaujeu later wrote that they were met by "an Indian nation of four hundred to five hundred members, dressed in skins of a kind of wild ox." The Indians turned out to be the Karankawas, and they were not friendly. They attacked La Salle's group with bows and arrows and killed three Frenchmen.

Father Hennepin drew this image of La Salle's fleet landing at Matagorda Bay, about eighty miles from present-day Galveston, Texas, in 1685. This trip deteriorated into a series of problems for the adventurers. They were lost, they had few supplies left, and many were sick and dying. But La Salle would not be deterred; despite the protests of his tired and hungry men, he vowed to journey on.

There were now 200 settlers left in La Salle's group. They moved their camp up a creek and began to set up a fort. They named their little camp Fort Saint Louis. The settlers were not experienced adventurers and weren't used to life without food and shelter. They lived in ragged tents made from cloth stretched over driftwood. They had no ovens, so they could not bake bread. Flour mixed with a little salt water was all they had to eat. Most of the crops they planted died in the hot, dry weather. Many of the chickens, cows, goats, and pigs they had brought with them got sick and died. Freshwater was hard to find, and many of the settlers grew sick. Five to six people died each day from hunger and disease. One of their best carpenters wandered away one day and never returned. Many of the settlers, including La Salle, were depressed.

Captain Beaujeu knew the settlers needed more food and medicine. He asked La Salle if he could take the *Joly* and sail to Martinique to get supplies. La Salle refused, but Beaujeu left anyway and returned to France. With the *Joly* gone, La Salle had just one small ship—the *Belle*—left.

La Salle and his men explored the area, and what they found did not lift their spirits. The discovery of an abandoned Spanish fort nearby worried them. They were afraid they would be attacked by the Spanish. In addition, the Native Americans in the area were not friendly. The settlers had to set fire to the grass around the fort to scare them off.

The Karankawas were hunters and gatherers. The name includes several bands of coastal people who shared a common language and culture. Karankawa is believed to mean "dog lovers" because they kept foxlike dogs. The Karankawa got food by hunting, fishing, and gathering. Fish, shellfish, and turtles were staples of their diet. They often smeared their bodies with a mixture of dirt and alligator or shark grease to ward off mosquitoes. The Karankawas did not understand the concept of private ownership and took whatever they needed. Not understanding Karankawan culture, Europeans considered them filthy, dangerous thieves.

For two years, La Salle and his group of settlers tried hard to set up a village. Life continued to be difficult for the little group. They hoped that Beaujeu would tell someone what had happened and send help. They did not realize that Beaujeu had returned to France. No one was looking for them.

At the end of October 1685, La Salle took about fifty men and went in search of the Mississippi. La Salle and some others rowed along the coast in small boats. The *Belle* followed them out in deeper water. La Salle later decided that the *Belle* didn't need to follow them. He ordered the *Belle*'s captain to bring the ship into deeper water and wait for him there.

La Salle continued along the coast and found some good land near a river. Although the river was not the Mississippi, La Salle realized it would be a better place for a camp. He decided to get the rest of the settlers and bring them back to the new camp in the *Belle*. Once again, La Salle was faced with a problem: He could not find the *Belle*. Some of the men remained to look for the lost ship while La Salle went back to Fort Saint Louis. He arrived in the middle of March 1686. The settlers were happy to see him. Then the rest of the men returned with the troubling news that the *Belle* had sunk. All their remaining supplies and all of La Salle's maps and notes were lost. More important, their only way to get back to France or get more supplies was now gone.

Stranded

This terrible news made La Salle sick once again. While he was recovering, he made a new plan. He decided he would try to find the Mississippi on foot. He believed that if he traveled north and east eventually he would find it. Then he could travel up the Mississippi to find help. On April 22, 1686, La Salle and twenty men set off. They crossed rivers and trudged over land. They met some Ceni Indians, who were very friendly and invited La Salle's group to stay with them for a few days. They met other friendly Native Americans who

Discovery of the *Belle*

When the *Belle* sank in Matagorda Bay in 1686, La Salle and his men never saw it again. But more than 300 years later, it was discovered by archaeologists off the coast of Texas. In 1995, they found the *Belle* buried under water and about twelve feet of sand. They were excited to find much of the ship still together. They also found cannons, plates, barrels, and tools. The ship and the things they found inside it gave scientists a good look at what life was like in La Salle's time.

The *Belle* is one of the most important shipwrecks ever discovered in North America. The excavation, shown above, was conducted in Matagorda Bay, Texas. It took a year and produced an amazing array of finds, including the hull of the ship, three cannons, thousands of glass beads, bronze hawk bells, pottery, and even the skeleton of a crew member. Every artifact found on the *Belle* has been identified, cleaned, and preserved. The hull of the ship has also been reconstructed and is being treated to preserve it.

gave them horses to make their journey easier. But La Salle and some others got sick again. They were forced to camp near a river for about two months while everyone recovered. By the end of the two months, they were almost out of gunpowder and bullets, and many men were still sick or had died. They headed back to Fort Saint Louis again.

They reached the fort in August. Only eight of the twenty men made it back. There were only about forty settlers left at the fort, and everyone was depressed. All, but La Salle, had given up hope.

Researchers excavating the *Belle* found the skull on the left in a rope locker. They made a plaster cast of it and used the skull's features to make a mold of what the person might have looked like.

La Salle was sick again and had to remain at Fort Saint Louis all through the fall while he recovered. At Christmas that year, the settlers sang songs and celebrated, but their situation was bad. Of the 287 people who had originally sailed from France, only thirty-seven were still alive. They had only the fort, some animals, a little cornmeal, some bullets and gunpowder, and a few cannons, but no cannonballs. They had no ship to sail for help and had no one to turn to.

La Salle and his crew were so hungry, they desperately searched for berries like these raspberries.

Early in January 1687, La Salle, Nika, La Salle's brother Jean Cavelier, and about sixteen other men set off on foot again in search of the Mississippi. The men did not have much food. They picked berries, killed buffalo when they could find them, and traded with Native Americans. The weather was bad, and they were often forced to stop and make tents out of buffalo skin where they could wait until the storm cleared. The cold, hungry, and tired men got into many fights with each other.

The End of La Salle's Journey

The group neared the Trinity River in eastern Texas, and La Salle remembered that he had hidden some corn nearby on a previous trip. He sent Nika and four other men to get the corn, but they found that the corn was ruined. On the way back to La Salle's camp, Nika shot two buffalo, and the men stopped to cut them up.

The next day, La Salle was worried when the men had not returned. He sent his nephew, Moranget, and three other men to look for them. When Moranget found Nika and the others, he got angry because they had already eaten the best parts of the buffalo. The men fought for a while, and after the fight ended, everyone went to sleep for the night. A man named Liotot was still angry, though. During the night, he killed Moranget, Nika, and La Salle's servant Saget.

Back at La Salle's camp, they were growing worried. Nika and the first group had not returned. Moranget and the second group also had not returned. La Salle and a priest named Anastase Douay went looking for the men. While they walked, La Salle told Douay that God had been very good to him and had looked out for him during his years of traveling. La Salle told Douay that he was very sad, and he did not know why.

This image illustrates the murder of La Salle by members of his expedition. La Salle provoked controversy both in his own lifetime and later. Those who knew him best praised his abilities. But his detractors, such as the survivors of his last expedition, felt he lacked leadership abilities and believed that his arrogance contributed to his death.

As they walked, La Salle and Douay saw some eagles in the sky and thought there might be a dead animal close by. La Salle fired two shots. The shots alerted the killers, who hid in the bushes. When La Salle and Douay got closer, one of the men stepped out of the bushes. La Salle asked where Moranget was, but the man didn't answer. Just then a man named Pierre Duhaut jumped out of the bushes and shot La Salle in the head. La Salle died instantly. The killers took off his clothes, dragged him into the bushes, and left him there. It was March 19, 1687, and La Salle was forty-three years old. His long journey was over.

What Happened to Everyone Else?

After shooting La Salle, the killers got into a fight with each other, and two more men were killed. The seven men who were still loyal to La Salle, including his brother, began walking in the direction of the Mississippi. They hoped to get back to Montreal. Although one of the men drowned in the Red River, the rest eventually got to Fort Saint Louis in Illinois, where Tonti was still waiting for

Henri de Tonti wrote about La Salle's expedition in his book, *An Account of Monsieur de la Salle's Last Expedition and Discoveries in North America*. Although La Salle was hampered by faults in his character and lacked the qualities of leadership, he possessed vision, tenacity, and courage. His claim of Louisiana for France pointed the way to the French colonial empire that was eventually built by other men.

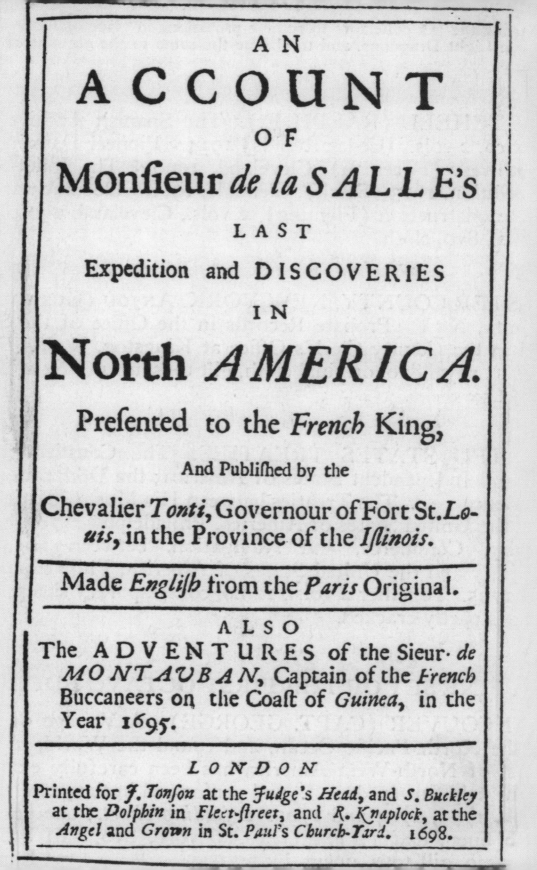

AN ACCOUNT

OF

Monsieur *de la* SALLE's

LAST

Expedition and DISCOVERIES

IN

North AMERICA.

Presented to the *French* King,

And Published by the

Chevalier *Tonti*, Governour of Fort St. *Louis*, in the Province of the *Islinois*.

Made *English* from the *Paris* Original.

ALSO

The ADVENTURES of the Sieur *de MONTAUBAN*, Captain of the *French* Buccaneers on the Coast of *Guinea*, in the Year 1695.

LONDON

Printed for *J. Tonson* at the *Judge's Head*, and *S. Buckley* at the *Dolphin* in *Fleet-street*, and *R. Knaplock*, at the *Angel* and *Crown* in St. *Paul's Church-Yard*. 1698.

La Salle. The men did not tell Tonti that La Salle had been killed. They needed to borrow money from him to get back to France. They were afraid he would not loan them money if he knew La Salle had been killed.

Tonti did not find out that La Salle was dead until two years after his murder. As soon as he found out, Tonti started down the Mississippi to try to find the settlers that had been left behind in Texas. Before he got there, he met some Native Americans. They told him the Spanish army was nearby. Tonti was forced to return to Fort Saint Louis near Lake Michigan.

Meanwhile, La Salle's little settlement in Texas was in ruins. The Karankawa Indians had killed most of the settlers. Some of the children were adopted by the Karankawas. A few years later, the Spanish discovered the children living with the Karankawas, but there was nothing left of Fort Saint Louis at Matagorda Bay.

6
THE LOUISIANA PURCHASE

The acquisition of . . . Louisiana is [very valuable], because . . . [it gives] us sole dominion [complete ownership] of the Mississippi.
   —Thomas Jefferson, describing the purchase of Louisiana

La Salle spent much of his life looking for and exploring the Mississippi. After claiming it for France and King Louis XIV, he died while trying to finalize his grand plan. What did King Louis XIV think of La Salle's claim of Louisiana? He was not very impressed with the Mississippi River or Louisiana. He did not see how either would be useful to him or to France.

France may not have been interested in their huge new land, but Spain was beginning to take an interest. The Spanish had explored Louisiana in the early 1500s but had established settlements only in Florida and Mexico. In the late 1500s, the English began exploring the east coast of North America, and Spain was forced to stay in Florida. They did not spend much time exploring the west.

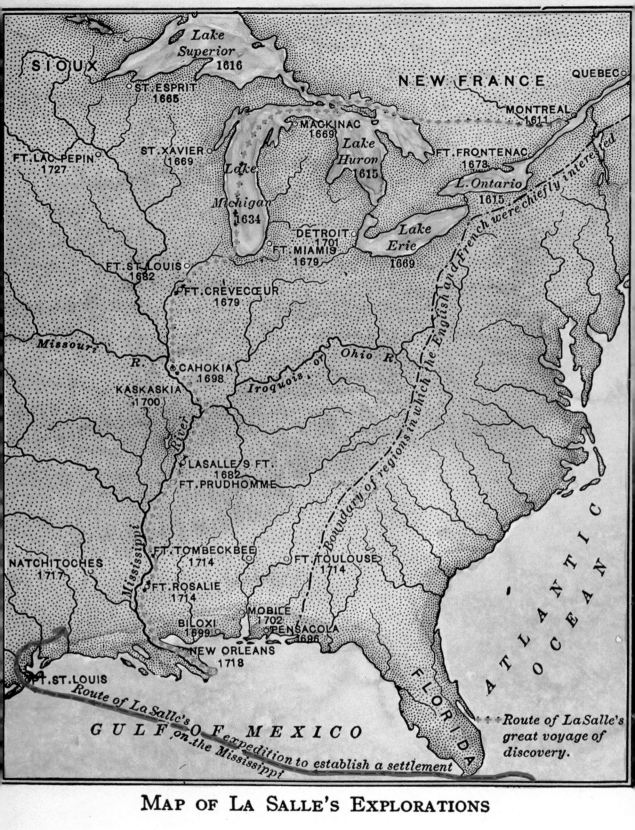

MAP OF LA SALLE'S EXPLORATIONS

That changed in September 1685 when the Spanish heard that La Salle was planning to set up a French colony at the end of the Mississippi. They realized they should begin exploring the land. They hoped to prevent other French settlers from coming. They gradually set up more villages in Florida, Texas, and Mexico.

John Law was a Scottish economist and banker who became infamous for the Mississippi Scheme, a colonial development project whose profits could not match the expectations stirred up by speculators.

The First Louisiana Settlements

It was not until seventeen years after La Salle claimed Louisiana that France finally began to try to settle people in the area. In April 1699, a small colony was established in Louisiana. England had begun to explore the Louisiana territory and France was not happy. France hoped

This map details the routes La Salle's expeditions took on each of his explorations. It also shows the locations and founding dates of various forts and settlements around the region.

the colony would remind England that the land belonged to France. But Louis XIV did not invest much money in the colony, and it did not do well.

France decided to try another settlement in Louisiana in 1716. King Louis XIV had died, and a man named John Law convinced the French government to spend money to develop Louisiana. Law formed the Company of the West. He got people to invest in the company, and he convinced others to move there. Originally only 500 people settled there, but within four years, there were more than 8,000. Life in the new colony wasn't easy, though. It was difficult to farm there, and many settlers died from disease and starvation. John Law's Company of the West went broke, and again France lost interest in Louisiana.

French settlers continued to live in Louisiana, however. In 1718, the city of New Orleans was established and more forts were built along the lower part of the Mississippi. France wanted to protect its land from the English and remind them that it was the owner of the land. The French made friends with the Native Americans to get help in protecting their forts against the English. But the French were soon to lose their hold on Louisiana.

The French and Indian War involved the struggle between Great Britain and France for control of North America. This painting illustrates British forces overcoming the French at Quiberon Bay in 1759. In this naval battle, off the southern coast of Brittany, France, the British destroyed the last French squadron in the Atlantic. The British were then able to stop French shipping and keep French troops out of Britain. This battle led to the Treaty of Paris in 1763. It gave Britain all of North America east of the Mississippi, including Florida. France gave up the western Mississippi valley to Spain as compensation for the loss of Florida. The French held most of the continent, from New Orleans to the Great Lakes and out to the Atlantic, but had managed to lose it to the British, who controlled only a thin strip along the Atlantic seaboard.

The French Leave Louisiana

The French and Indian War (also known as the Seven Years' War) began in 1754. The English were eager to expand north and west into land owned by France. France was determined not to let that happen, but they lost the war. In 1763, they were forced to give up their land in North America. England got Canada and Louisiana east of the Mississippi (except for the city of New Orleans). Spain had helped France during the war, and they had lost Florida as a result. To repay them, France gave Spain the area of Louisiana west of the Mississippi and New Orleans.

War soon changed things again. The English colonists had been fighting with England to win their independence. In 1783, the Revolutionary War ended and the United States was born. The United States was now made up of the thirteen colonies and Louisiana east of the Mississippi. Florida was returned to Spain by England.

The young country of the United States was eager to expand west. They wanted control of the rest of Louisiana. They also realized something that La Salle had known years before: The Mississippi was a very important river. This was especially true for the colonists who lived west of the Appalachian Mountains. It was much easier for them to ship goods down the Mississippi to New Orleans and then to Europe than it was to haul the goods over the mountains to the east coast.

The great French emperor Napoleon had a hand in forming the United States. Worried that the fledgling United States would attack Louisiana, in 1803 he agreed to sell to America the land France owned for $15 million. This is known as the Louisiana Purchase.

Unfortunately for the United States, Spain still controlled New Orleans and the lower Mississippi. They allowed Americans to trade there, but the two countries did not always get along. Spain realized that they were spending too much money to keep things running in New Orleans. By 1800, they wanted to get rid of it. America was very interested in getting New Orleans, but things were getting complicated.

In 1799, Napoleon Bonaparte (1769–1821) became unofficial dictator of France. He wanted to get Louisiana back under French control. He began negotiating with Spain

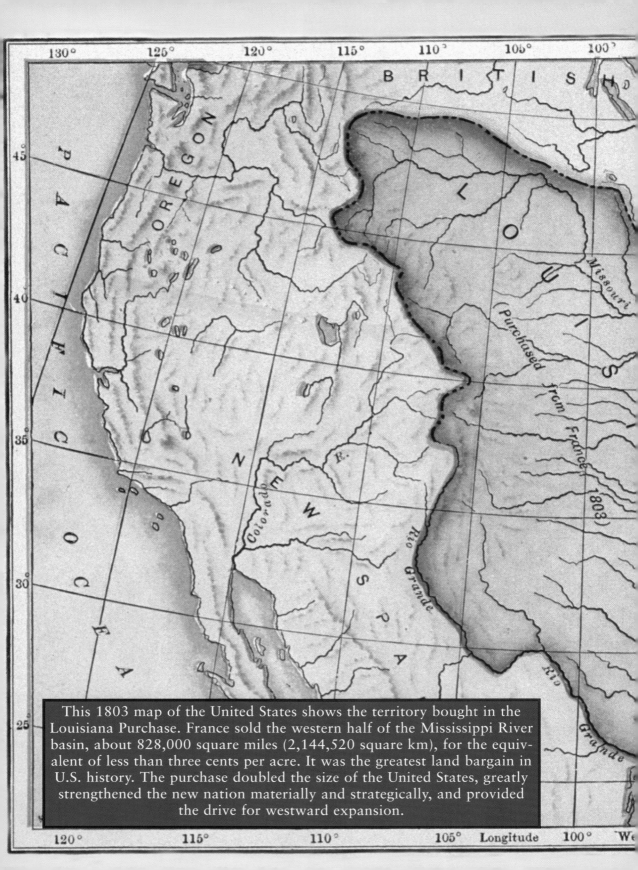

This 1803 map of the United States shows the territory bought in the Louisiana Purchase. France sold the western half of the Mississippi River basin, about 828,000 square miles (2,144,520 square km), for the equivalent of less than three cents per acre. It was the greatest land bargain in U.S. history. The purchase doubled the size of the United States, greatly strengthened the new nation materially and strategically, and provided the drive for westward expansion.

about gaining control of their part of Louisiana. On October 1, 1800, France and Spain agreed to a trade. France got Louisiana and six warships. Spain got the part of Italy that was controlled by France.

America Plans to Buy Louisiana

It wasn't until a year later that anyone in America found out about the agreement between France and Spain. Thomas Jefferson was president of the United States. The fact that France again owned

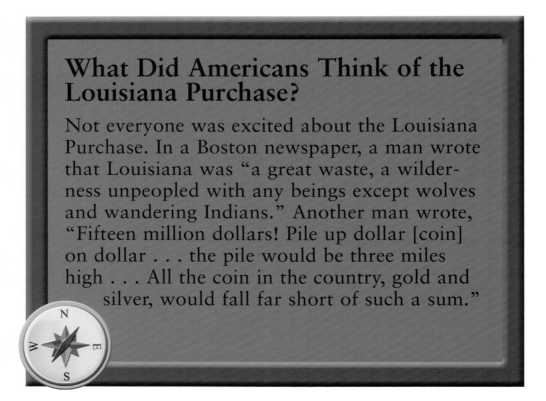

What Did Americans Think of the Louisiana Purchase?

Not everyone was excited about the Louisiana Purchase. In a Boston newspaper, a man wrote that Louisiana was "a great waste, a wilderness unpeopled with any beings except wolves and wandering Indians." Another man wrote, "Fifteen million dollars! Pile up dollar [coin] on dollar . . . the pile would be three miles high . . . All the coin in the country, gold and silver, would fall far short of such a sum."

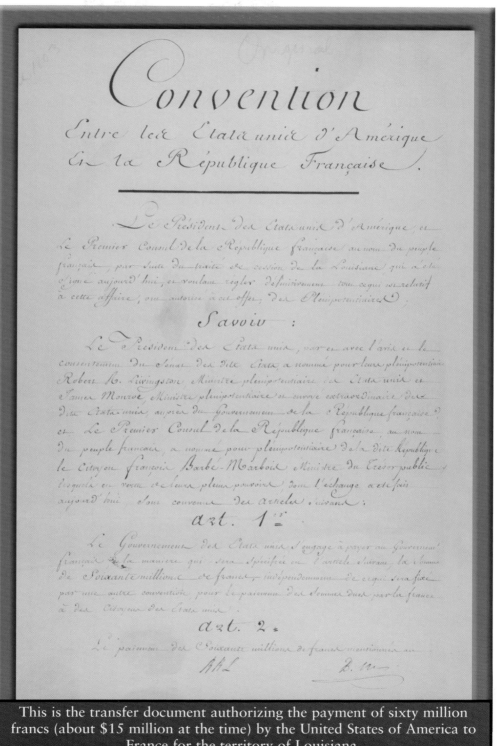

This is the transfer document authorizing the payment of sixty million francs (about $15 million at the time) by the United States of America to France for the territory of Louisiana.

part of Louisiana worried him. He dreamed of America being one country, ruled by one government. He tried to buy New Orleans and French Louisiana, but France did not want to sell. Jefferson persisted.

After two years, Napoleon finally agreed to sell the land France owned to America. France needed money and Napoleon also worried that America would attack Louisiana. In July 1803, Jefferson got the good news that France had agreed to sell Louisiana for $15 million. America got New Orleans, all other land owned by France, and all public buildings on the land. America had to borrow money from banks in Europe to pay France. Over time, they paid an extra $11 million in interest. Still, they paid only five cents per acre for French Louisiana. The Louisiana Purchase, as it is now known, almost doubled the size of the United States.

Lewis and Clark Explore the New Land

President Jefferson knew that America had made a great deal when it bought Louisiana. However, he was not sure exactly what they now had. He decided to send Meriwether Lewis and William Clark to find out. Lewis and Clark left Saint

The expedition of Captain Meriwether Lewis and Lieutenant William Clark was the first overland expedition of the United States. They went from St. Louis to the Pacific Coast and back from 1804 to 1806. In this image, Lewis and Clark are accompanied by Sacajawea, the Shoshone Indian woman who, carrying her infant son on her back, traveled thousands of miles guiding the expedition through the wilderness areas of the West.

Louis on May 14, 1804. They spent the next two and a half years exploring the vast land that La Salle had claimed for France more than one hundred years earlier. Lewis and Clark did not find the waterway to the Pacific that La Salle had dreamed about. They did find the beautiful land filled with plants, birds, and animals that Native Americans had treasured for centuries.

The Mississippi and the Louisiana Purchase Today

The Mississippi River proved to be very important to America. By the mid-1800s, riverboats carried loads of corn, wheat, and tobacco from the fields of the Midwest. Lumber and fur from the forests were hauled to the cities. Sugar, cotton, and whiskey from other countries traveled up the river. The Mississippi remains an important trade and transportation route. Today, huge barges still carry millions of tons of cargo up and down the river.

The land included in the Louisiana Purchase also proved to be very valuable. Gold and silver were discovered in areas. The forests and farmlands have provided food and timber for the entire country.

La Salle faced many difficulties during his life, but he never gave up. Even when others doubted him and conditions were dismal, he kept trying to make his dreams come true. Although he never succeeded in setting up a French empire along the Mississippi, La Salle's faith in the importance of the Mississippi proved right.

The Mississippi River has evolved from La Salle's time to become one of the busiest commercial waterways in the world. Additionally, the river has inspired unique contributions to the history and literature of the United States. Stories and legends about the river are a vital part of the folklore and national consciousness of Americans.

CHRONOLOGY

November 21, 1643 René-Robert Cavelier, Sieur de La Salle, is born in Rouen, France.

1667 La Salle leaves the Jesuits and moves to Montreal, Canada.

1669–1673 La Salle explores the Great Lakes region.

1677 La Salle returns to France to get permission to search for the Mississippi River.

1678–1679 La Salle builds the *Griffon* and sets sail August 7, 1679.

1679 La Salle begins the trip down the Saint Joseph River in search of the Mississippi.

1680 The *Griffon* is lost; Fort Crèvecoeur is built.

1681 La Salle returns to Montreal for more men and supplies.

February 13, 1682   Mississippi journey begins.

April 9, 1682   La Salle claims the Mississippi River and all surrounding land for France.

1683   La Salle returns to France to report his claim.

March 1684   Louis XIV agrees to help finance another expedition.

July 24, 1684   La Salle sets sail for the Gulf of Mexico with four ships and misses the Mississippi River.

February 1685   Fort Saint Louis is established in Texas.

1686–1687   La Salle tries to find the Mississippi on foot.

March 19, 1687   La Salle is killed by Pierre Duhaut.

April 1699   First French colony is established in Louisiana.

1763   France loses the French and Indian War and has to give Louisiana to Spain.

1800   France gets Louisiana back from Spain.

1803   United States buys Louisiana from France for $15 million.

GLOSSARY

ammunition   Bullets, cannonballs, or other explosives used for defense.

archaeologist   A person who studies prehistorical human life by examining artifacts.

astronomy   The study of the sun, stars, and planets.

barge   A large flat-bottomed boat that is used to transport goods in waterways.

cargo   Goods loaded on a boat.

contract   A legal agreement between two people or groups.

convert   To persuade someone to practice a new religion.

debt   Money owed to someone else.

engineer   A person trained in the design and construction of machines.

geography   The study of the earth.

global positioning system (GPS)   A system of satellites that provides precise locations.

grenade A small explosive.

interest A fee charged for borrowing money.

Jesuit A member of a religious group of Roman Catholic priests.

landmark A specific feature of land that serves as a guide.

marsh Low, wet land, usually with few trees.

meteoric Very quick.

mill A building where grain is ground into flour.

mine A hole in the ground dug to reach a deposit of minerals.

missionary A person sent by a church to convert people to their religion.

mythical Imaginary.

navigation The planning of a route.

peace pipe A tobacco pipe smoked during a ceremony as a sign of friendship.

plain Flat land.

settlement A small community or village.

stake A thin pole.

territory The land or water belonging to a state or government.

treaty A formal agreement sometimes signed to establish peace.

whaler A ship used to capture whales.

FOR MORE INFORMATION

The Mariners' Museum
100 Museum Drive
Newport News, VA 23606
(757) 596-2222
Web site: http://www.mariner.org

Maritime Park Association
P.O. Box 470310
San Francisco, CA 94147-0310
(415) 561-6662
Web site: http://www.maritime.org

Due to the changing nature of Internet links, the Rosen Publishing Group, Inc., has developed an online list of Web sites related to the subject of this book. This site is updated regularly. Please use this link to access the list: http://www.rosenlinks.com/lee/lasa/

FOR FURTHER READING

Bergen, Lara. *The Travels of Sieur de La Salle*. Austin, TX: Raintree/Steck-Vaughn Publishers, 2001.

Blumberg, Rhoda. *What's the Deal? Jefferson, Napoleon, and the Louisiana Purchase*. Washington, DC: National Geographic Society, 1998.

Corrick, James A. *The Louisiana Purchase*. San Diego: Lucent Books, 2001.

Coulter, Tony. *La Salle and the Explorers of the Mississippi*. New York: Chelsea House Publishers, 1991.

Hargrove, Jim. *The World's Great Explorers: René-Robert Cavelier Sieur de La Salle*. Chicago, IL: Childrens Press, 1990.

Jacobs, William Jay. *La Salle: Life of Boundless Adventure*. New York: Franklin Watts, 1994.

BIBLIOGRAPHY

Bitterli, Urs. *Cultures in Conflict: Encounters Between European and Non-European Cultures, 1492–1800.* Stanford, CA: Stanford University Press, 1986.

Galloway, Patricia, ed. *La Salle and His Legacy: Frenchmen and Indians in the Lower Mississippi Valley.* Jackson, MS: University Press of Mississippi, 1982.

Nash, Gary B. *Red, White and Black: The Peoples of Early North America,* Fourth Edition. Upper Saddle River, NJ: Prentice Hall, 2000.

Spurr, Daniel. *River of Forgotten Days: A Journey Down the Mississippi in Search of La Salle.* New York: Henry Holt and Company, 1998.

Weddle, Robert S., ed. *La Salle, the Mississippi, and the Gulf: Three Primary Documents.* College Station, TX: Texas A & M University Press, 1987.

Weddle, Robert S. *Wilderness Manhunt: The Spanish Search for La Salle.* Austin, TX: University of Texas Press, 1973.

INDEX

About the Author

Simone Payment has a degree in psychology from Cornell University and a master's degree in elementary education from Wheelock College. She has taught elementary school, worked in book publishing, and currently works for a health care company. She is also the author of *Buck Leonard* in the Rosen Publishing Group's Baseball Hall of Famers of the Negro Leagues series.

Acknowledgments

The author would like to thank Lori Cooper and Marina Lang for their suggestions and support.

Photo Credits

Series Design and Layout

Tahara Hasan

Editor

Christine Poolos